Wash Your Hands

By Lilith Dollard
Illustrated by Marjolein Francois

Library For All Ltd.

Library For All is an Australian not for profit organisation with a mission to make knowledge accessible to all via an innovative digital library solution. Visit us at libraryforall.org

Wash Your Hands

This edition published 2022

Published by Library For All Ltd
Email: info@libraryforall.org
URL: libraryforall.org

Library For All gratefully acknowledges the contributions of all who made previous editions of this book possible.

Original illustrations by Marjolein Francois

Wash Your Hands
Dollard, Lilith
ISBN: 978-1-922827-73-9
SKU02667

Wash Your Hands

Wash your hands
in the morning.

Wash your hands
before breakfast.

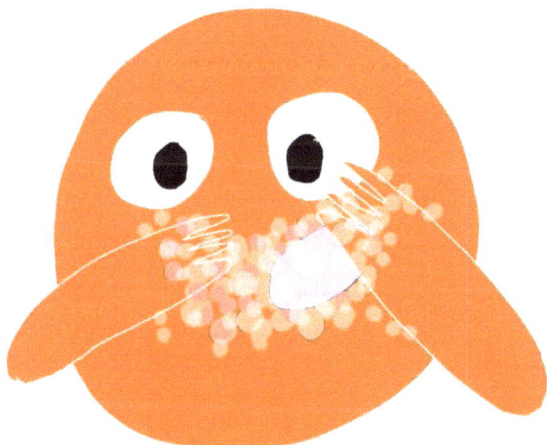
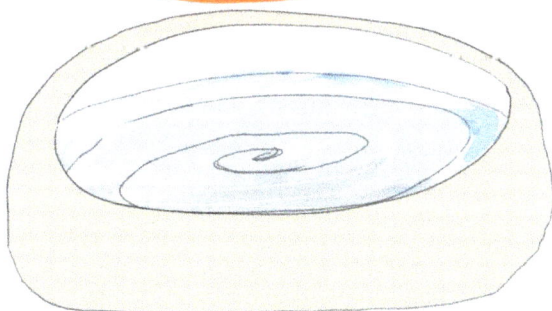

Wash your hands
after breakfast.

Wash your hands
at school.

Wash your hands
after playing
outside.

Wash your hands
before lunch.

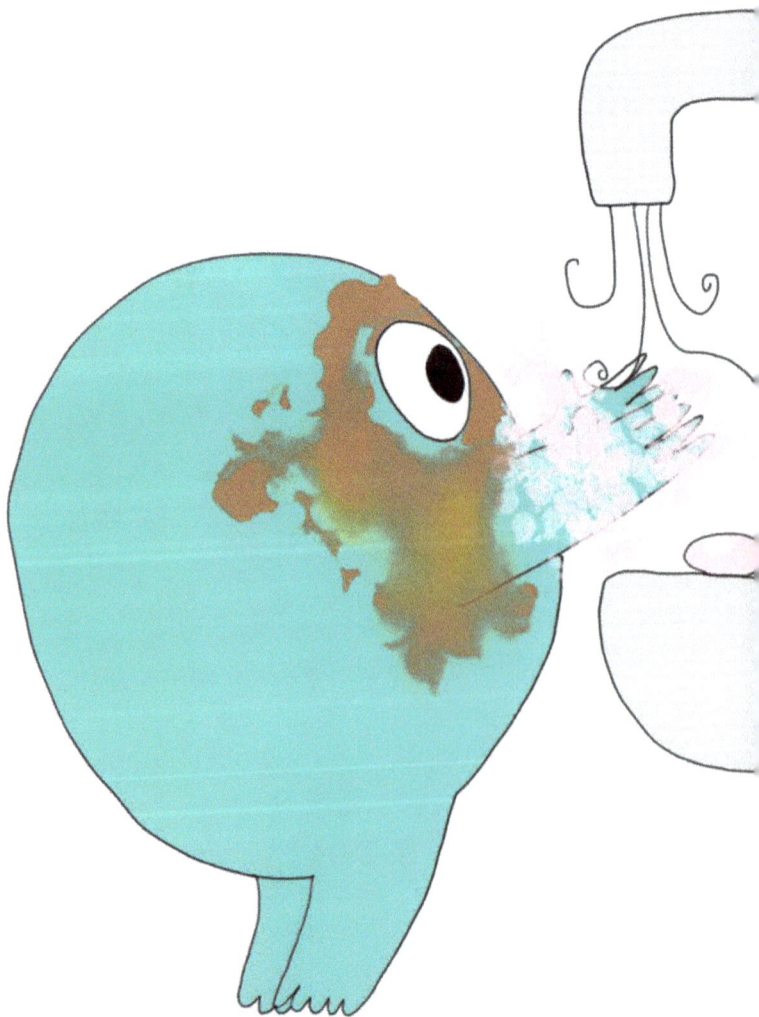

Wash your hands
after lunch.

Wash your hands after using the toilet.

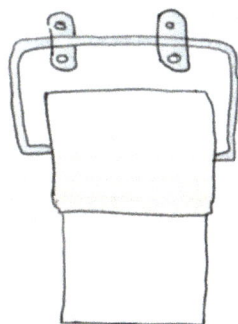

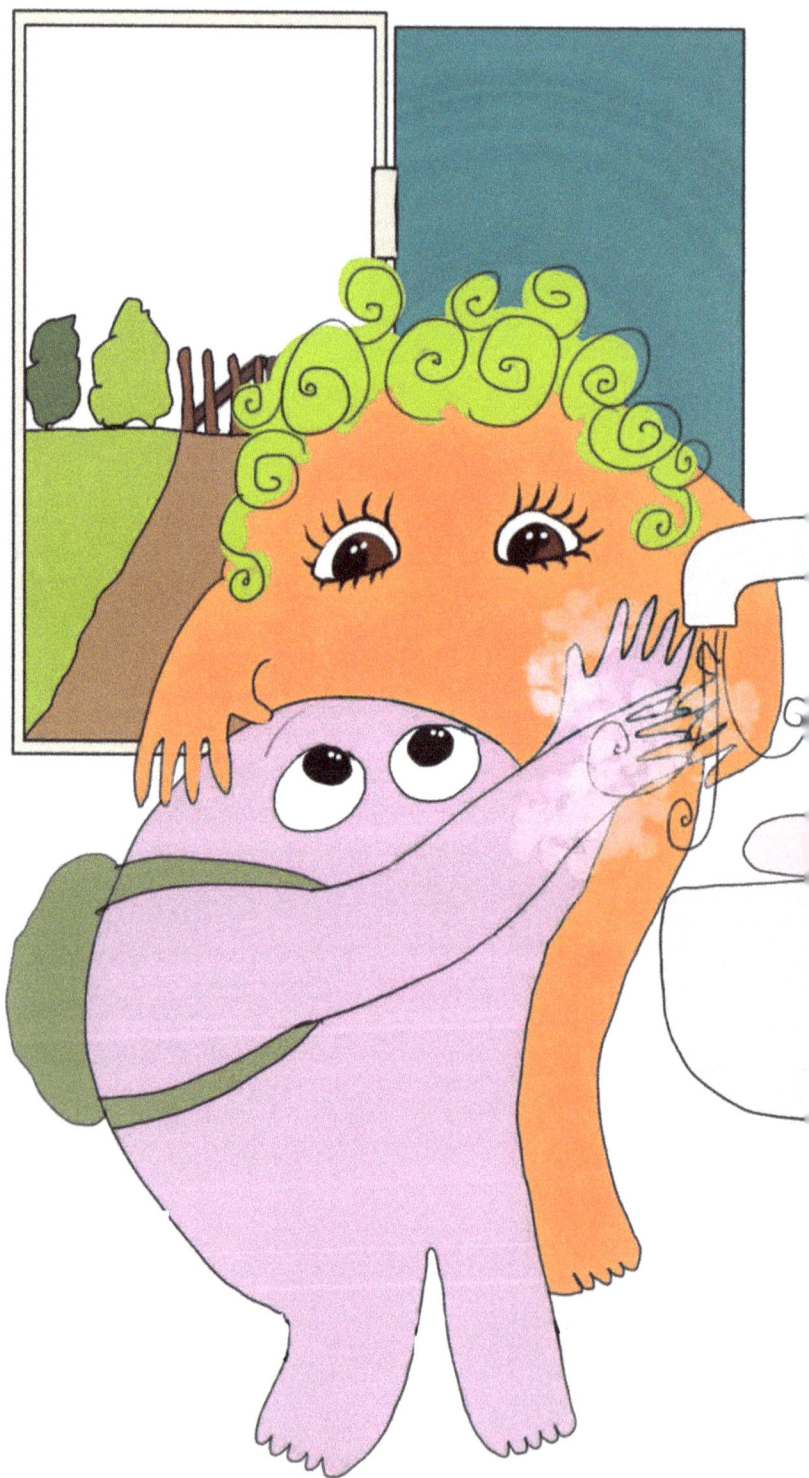

Wash your hands when you get home.

Wash your hands
before dinner.

Wash your hands
after dinner.

Wash your hands
before you go to
sleep.

25

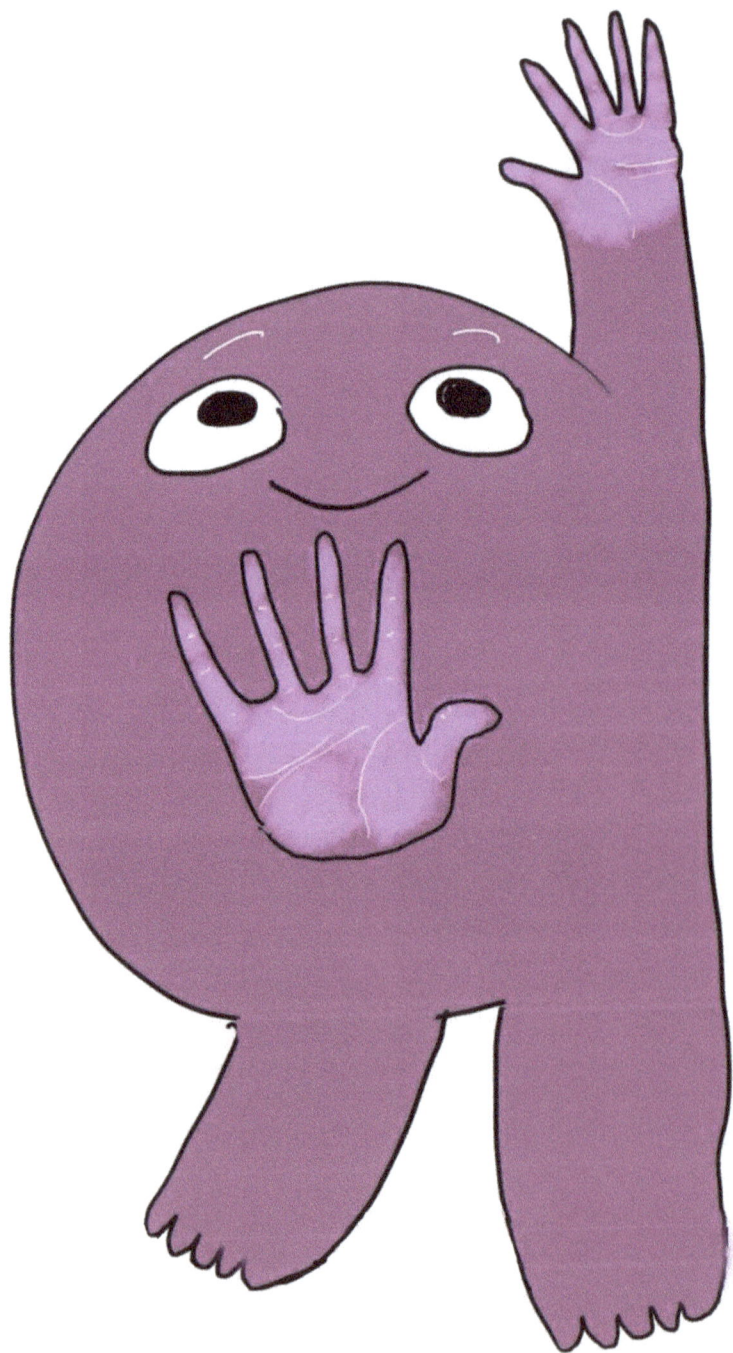

Wash your hands
to stay healthy
and happy!

You can use these questions to talk about this book with your family, friends and teachers.

What did you learn from this book?

Describe this book in one word. Funny? Scary? Colourful? Interesting?

How did this book make you feel when you finished reading it?

What was your favourite part of this book?

About the contributors

Library For All works with authors and illustrators from around the world to develop diverse, relevant, high quality stories for young readers. Visit libraryforall.org for the latest news on writers' workshop events, submission guidelines and other creative opportunities.

Did you enjoy this book?

We have hundreds more expertly curated original stories to choose from.

We work in partnership with authors, educators, cultural advisors, governments and NGOs to bring the joy of reading to children everywhere.

Did you know?

We create global impact in these fields by embracing the United Nations Sustainable Development Goals.